The Case of the Ancient Artefact

Samuel Sheehy

Burlington Books

The Case of the Ancient Artefact

by Samuel Sheehy

Burlington Books
P. O. Box 54411
3721 Limassol
Cyprus
Burlington Books is an imprint of the Burlington Group.

The publisher gratefully acknowledges the following for providing photographs:
© Alamy: page 55; © Archivo de El Museo Canario: cover, pages 7 (*pintadera*), 23; © Shutterstock.com: pages 7 (all except Mona Lisa and *pintadera*), 22, 31, 46, 54, 62, 63, 64; © Visipix: page 7 (Mona Lisa)

The publisher would like to thank the following people:
Castellano: Mónica de la Riva de la Rosa
Català: Maria Esteve Serraviñals
Euskara: Edurne Azkue Urrestilla
Galego: Ramón Nicolás Rodríguez

ISBN 978-9963-51-261-4

Burlington Reader No. NE3.14

10 9 8 7
24 23 22

CONTENTS

Introducción

Dos historiadores se encargan de llevar un valioso objeto desde Canarias hasta Londres para una gran exposición. Unos granujas tienen conocimiento de ello y pretenden hacerse con él. Carlota, una confiada joven de 20 años, viaja a Londres en el mismo avión. Las cosas se complican cuando roban el tesoro y este termina en el bolso de Carlota. Sin saberlo, lo lleva a Londres y entonces comienzan los problemas para ella. Los historiadores quieren recuperar el valioso objeto ya que el museo lo necesita como principal atracción de la exposición. Los ladrones, por su parte, están decididos a robarlo y no se detendrán ante nada. Carlota corre gran peligro. ¿Conseguirá salir de este lío?

Introducció

Dos historiadors s'encarreguen de portar un valuós objecte des de les Canàries fins a Londres per a una gran exposició. Uns bandarres en tenen coneixement i pretenen aconseguir-lo. La Carlota, una confiada jove de vint anys, viatja cap a Londres en el mateix avió. Les coses es compliquen quan roben el tresor i aquest acaba dins la bossa de la Carlota. Sense saber-ho, el porta a Londres i llavors comencen els problemes per a ella. Els historiadors volen recuperar el valuós objecte, ja que el museu el necessita com a principal atracció de l'exposició. Els lladres, per la seva banda, estan decidits a robar-lo i res no els aturarà. La Carlota corre un gran perill. Aconseguirà sortir-se'n d'aquest embolic?

Sarrera

Objektu baliotsu bat Kanarietatik Londresera erakusketa batera eramatearen ardura hartu dute bi historialarik. Gizatxar batzuek horren berri dute, eta lapurtzen saiatuko dira. Carlota, 20 urteko gazte fidakorra, hegazkin berean doa Londresera. Gauzak nahasten hasiko dira altxorra lapurtzen dutenean eta Carlotaren poltsan bukatzen duenean. Jakin gabe, Carlotak Londresera eramango du, eta orduan hasiko dira arazoak neskarentzat. Historialariek objektu baliotsua berreskuratu nahi dute, museoak behar baitu, erakusketako izar nagusia delako. Lapurrek, aldiz, garbi dute ostu nahi dutela, eta ezerk ez ditu geldiaraziko. Carlota arrisku handian dago. Lortuko ote du nahaspila horretatik irtetea?

Limiar

Dous historiadores encárganse de levar un valioso obxecto desde Canarias até Londres para unha grande exposición. Uns pillabáns teñen coñecemento diso e perseguen facerse con el. Carlota, unha confiada moza de 20 anos, viaxa a Londres no mesmo avión. As cousas complícanse cando rouban o tesouro e este remata no bolso de Carlota. Sen sabelo, lévao a Londres e daquela comezan os problemas para ela. Os historiadores queren recuperar o valioso obxecto pois o museo vai precisalo como principal atracción da exposición. Os ladróns, pola súa banda, están decididos a roubalo e non se deterán diante de nada. Carlota corre gran perigo. Poderá saír desta lea?

THE CHARACTERS

PRE-READING ACTIVITIES

1 Complete the text with the words below.

sketches *valuable* *steal* *research* *ancient*

My brother works in the history department of the university. He does 1. .... on the 2. .... items there to discover how people lived thousands of years ago. First, he makes 3. .... of the items and then he studies them. There are guards in the university because the items are very 4. .... and thieves sometimes try to 5. .... them.

2 Tick (✓) the items you can see on display in a museum.

a

b

c

d

e

f

g

CHAPTER 1

At the Airport

In the departure hall of Las Palmas airport in Gran Canaria, two men were walking together. They looked like businessmen, dressed in elegant suits. One of the men was Professor Manuel Toledo, a famous historian. He was walking with his assistant, a student called Tomás Silva.

"We'll meet a lot of important people at the museum in London," said Professor Toledo. "If we're lucky, somebody will really enjoy the exhibition and give us money to continue our **research**."

"I hope so," said Tomás. "We need to **raise funds**, so we can continue excavating on the Canary Islands."

"Don't worry. People will see the *pintadera* collection, and then they'll understand the importance of our work," said the professor. Tomás didn't say anything. He was very nervous about the exhibition as it was his responsibility. This was his first exhibition abroad and the British Museum was an important museum. It received more than six million visitors a year. This was their big opportunity to get some great publicity.

"Is the *pintadera* safe?" asked the professor. "Which bag did you put it in?"

"Don't worry, it's right here," said Tomás. He took a small object from his bag. It was **wrapped** in a piece of soft **leather**.

Tomás opened the leather to check the small, round ceramic ornament inside. There was a picture of a sun, made from triangles and circles. It was very old and valuable. Tomás held it very carefully.

"It looks more beautiful every time I see it," said Professor Toledo. "Did you know that this is the oldest example of a *pintadera* in the world?"

"Yes, of course I know that, I'm not stupid!" said Tomás, carefully wrapping the ornament in its cover and putting it in his bag again. He felt a little insulted. It was not the first time he felt that the professor didn't respect him. Tomás wanted to be a professor himself. "Then, people will take me seriously," he thought. "They'll understand that I'm also an excellent historian."

Tomás opened the leather to check the small, round ceramic ornament inside.

They still had some time before boarding, so the two men sat down. Professor Toledo began to read a book about the history of the Canary Islands, his favourite subject. Tomás took a cheese sandwich from his bag and began to eat it. Time passed and he was bored. They still had a long time until boarding.

"I'll go and have a walk around the duty-free shops," he said to Professor Toledo. "Do you need anything?"

"No, I'm reading!" the professor answered, impatiently. He was irritated. "Why do you want to **waste** your time there?"

"Because I'm bored," Tomás said. "I'm sorry to **disturb** you."

Tomás entered the brightly coloured shop and looked around him. It was full of people. There was a problem with the air-conditioning and it was hot in the shop. Tomás removed his jacket and put it, with his bag, in the **trolley**. He went over to the electronics **counter** and checked out the selection of mobile phones there. Tomás loved mobile phones and could talk for ages about all the different models and their characteristics. There were special offers on a few of the latest models, and Tomás couldn't resist a **bargain**. Neither could the other passengers. They pushed around him, trying to see all the bargains.

Soon, he was **deep in** discussion with the salesman about all the new mobile phones on offer. The salesman was very convincing, and before he knew it, Tomás was buying a new phone. He was very pleased with himself – it was much cheaper than the shops in his home town. He couldn't wait to use it.

The salesman was very convincing, and before he knew it, Tomás was buying a new phone.

The **queue** to pay was long and Tomás continued adding bargain items to his trolley – chocolate, deodorant and a magazine. It was more interesting than sitting with the professor. Finally, it was his turn to pay and leave the shop.

Tomás returned to his seat next to Professor Toledo. The professor was still busy reading his book. Tomás checked his watch. Not long to go now. He took out his new phone and started to download his favourite apps.

CHAPTER 2

A Visit to England

In the food area outside the duty-free shops, 20-year-old Carlota was drinking her iced coffee and watching the passengers around her. It was a very hot day outside but the food area was air-conditioned and cool. It was a pity to leave Gran Canaria during such a hot summer. Carlota lived in the south of the island next to a beautiful beach, and she was going to **miss** swimming and sunbathing with her friends. But then she remembered why she was going to London – to visit her sister María, her sister's husband and their new baby. Carlota was very excited about meeting her sweet little niece, but she felt bad that she wasn't going to watch her grow up because she lived far away.

"Excuse me. Is anybody sitting here?" asked a well-dressed man in a grey shirt and shiny black shoes. He was older than Carlota, maybe in his thirties, and he was very handsome. He had dark brown hair and nice eyes. He was slim, and had a warm smile. Carlota smiled back.

"No. Nobody's sitting there," she said.

"Thank you," said the man. He sat down opposite her and put a small cup of espresso on the table. "My name is Julio," he said. Carlota told him her name and tried not to stare at him.

"That's a pretty name," said Julio. "It's perfect for a pretty woman like you."

Carlota was **embarrassed** and didn't know what to say. She liked the look of the man, but his comment made her feel uncomfortable.

"I'm sorry," he said. "You've gone red. I didn't mean to embarrass you."

"It's OK," said Carlota. "Where are you flying to?" she asked, trying to change the subject.

"I'm flying to Paris for a business meeting," said Julio, and he told her all about his job as a **property developer**. It sounded very interesting. Carlota told him about her new niece in London. She enjoyed the conversation and forgot about her embarrassment before.

Carlota enjoyed the conversation and forgot about her embarrassment before.

"So, you're leaving on the next flight to London?" Julio asked her.

"Yes," answered Carlota. "We're boarding in about 15 minutes."

"But I think there was an announcement for passengers on the London flight," said Julio. "I wasn't really listening, but I think there's a delay or something. Didn't you hear it?"

Carlota started to panic. "No! I didn't hear anything," she said, worried. "Maybe they announced it when I was in the bathroom."

"There's an information board just over there," said Julio, pointing to an area not far from them. "You can check your flight information. Go on, I'll watch your bags for you."

"Thank you," said Carlota. She went to the board and checked the data for the London flight. *"Flight IB 3476. Boarding ten minutes. Gate 11."*

Carlota went to the board and checked the data for the London flight.

Very happy, she returned to the handsome Julio. "You were mistaken, the delay wasn't on the London flight," she told him, with a smile. "My flight is on time. I'm boarding in ten minutes. Thanks for watching my bags."

"You're welcome," said Julio. "Now you should run for your plane. You don't want to miss it. But maybe I'll see you again in Gran Canaria, one day."

"I hope so," said Carlota, going red again. "Enjoy Paris."

"Thanks," said Julio, with a warm smile. "Enjoy London, and especially being with your niece!"

Reluctantly, Carlota said goodbye to her new friend, took her bags and went to join the passengers standing in the queue for boarding.

CHAPTERS 1-2 ACTIVITIES

1 Circle six words in the puzzle. Then use the words to complete the sentences below.

excitedcoverhandsomeuncomfortableworriedstaring

1. She's .... because it's late and her son isn't home yet.
2. Why are you .... at me? Is something wrong?
3. My face went red when the .... man smiled at me.
4. I bought a new .... for my mobile phone.
5. Most people feel .... when you look at them for a long time.
6. The children were very .... because it was their first trip abroad.

2 Tick (✓) the sentences true (T) or false (F). Pay attention to the words in bold.

	T	F
1. A **passenger** gives people food in a café.		
2. Your sister's daughter is your **niece**.		
3. **Embarrassment** is a negative feeling.		
4. **Departure** is the act of leaving a place.		
5. A married woman can't have a **husband**.		
6. Before you go on a **flight**, you must learn how to fly.		

Did you know?

Sir Hans Sloane's collection of 71,000 objects was used to start the British Museum in 1753. Today, the museum has got over eight million objects.

3 Match the questions to the answers.

Questions

1. Why were the two men travelling to London?
2. Why was Tomás nervous?
3. Why was the *pintadera* important?
4. Why did Carlota feel uncomfortable with Julio at first?
5. Why did Carlota leave Julio to watch her bags?
6. Why didn't Julio board the plane with Carlota?

Answers

.... a. Because he was flying to Paris.

.... b. Because he gave Carlota a compliment.

.... c. Because he offered to watch her bags while she checked the flight board.

.... d. Because it was his first exhibition abroad.

.... e. Because people would enjoy seeing it and give money for more research on ancient items.

.... f. Because they were attending an exhibition.

4 Answer the questions. Write the answers in your notebook.

1. What was Tomás' attitude towards the professor?
2. Why was the professor rude to Tomás?
3. What did Tomás decide to do while the professor was reading?
4. What was the purpose of Carlota's trip?
5. Who did Carlota meet while she was waiting for her flight?

CHAPTER 3

Arriving in London

Holding her map, Carlota stood at the bus stop and tried to understand her sister's instructions. This was only Carlota's second visit to London and she couldn't remember her way around the city. María wanted to meet her sister at the airport, but Carlota thought she could find her own way. Now she was sorry.

Carlota looked at the map and then again at María's instructions. Then, she looked back at the confusing numbers on the bus stop sign. An elderly woman was watching her carefully. She could see that Carlota was confused.

"Where are you trying to get to?" asked the woman, kindly.

"Get to?" asked Carlota. Normally, she could speak English very well, but she felt nervous because she was lost and she didn't understand the question.

"Where are you trying to get to?" asked the woman, kindly.

"Where do you want to go?" asked the woman, moving closer. Carlota showed the woman María's address on the small piece of paper. The woman looked at it.

"This is the right bus stop," she said. "You must take the number 2 bus to the big shopping centre. It will come in ten minutes. Then get off and get on a different bus. The number 14 bus will take you to this street."

"Thank you very much," said Carlota, smiling. She was proud that she was finding her way. As Carlota was waiting for the bus, it started to rain. "Typical English weather," she thought. "It's sunny one minute and raining the next!" When the bus came, she sat on a seat next to the window. She repeated to herself, "Shopping centre, number 14 bus," to help her remember the instructions.

As the bus doors closed, two men tried to get on, but the bus driver didn't stop. Angrily, they **banged on** the windows and shouted at him. Their hair and clothes were wet from the rain. Carlota felt bad for them, but she didn't like the way they were shouting and screaming. As the bus started to move away, Carlota observed the men. She couldn't be sure, but she thought that one of them was pointing at her. She turned her back and tried to forget them. "Shopping centre, number 14 bus," she said to herself.

Gary Smith and George Kelly were sitting in a car outside the airport. Suddenly, Gary's phone rang. It was their partner, Julio.

"Are you in place?" he asked.

"Yes, we're outside the arrivals, watching the passengers," answered Gary. "Were you successful?"

"Yes, it was very simple," Julio replied. "There was quite a **crowd** in the duty free and the historian didn't see me take the *pintadera* from his bag. He made it easy for me ... he left it in his trolley and was busy talking to the salesman! After that, I put it into a young girl's bag. She's got no idea it's in there."

"Well, it won't be there much longer," said Gary. "We'll get it from her, don't worry. Describe her to us."

Twenty minutes later, the men were still waiting for the young Spanish woman to appear. They knew that she was pretty, and had long dark hair. They knew she was wearing blue jeans and a purple top, with maybe a coat now because of the weather. Most important, she was carrying a red bag. And in that bag, hopefully, was the small but very valuable piece of art called a *pintadera*.

At last, Carlota appeared. She was leaving the airport and moving to the bus waiting outside. They knew it was her. She had the red bag over her shoulder. She was also pulling a large, heavy suitcase. They followed the bus closely in the car. They hoped to take the bag quickly, without hurting the girl.

They followed the bus for a long way. At last, it stopped on a busy street and they saw Carlota get off. She was holding a map and looking a bit lost. She started to speak to a lady, clearly asking about the buses. They could get the bag now! George tried to park the car, but there was no space and there was a police car behind them. They had no option. "Oh no! Now we'll have to drive around that corner to find parking!"

It took some minutes to find parking and they were very agitated by now. It was raining heavily as they quickly ran back to the bus stop. But when they arrived, the bus doors were closing!

"Stop the bus!" shouted Gary, and he hit the doors.

"Open the doors!" shouted George, but the driver didn't stop. The bus left, taking Carlota and the *pintadera* with it.

"Open the doors!" shouted George, but the driver didn't stop.

CHAPTER 4

A Surprise Attack

"But I don't understand!" cried Tomás, the historian. "I had it in my bag! You saw it!" He looked at Professor Toledo, paralysed with fear.

The professor looked at Tomás with irritation. "What an irresponsible idiot," he was thinking. "I can't believe this. The people at the museum will be furious."

The two men were talking to two policemen at Heathrow Airport. They discovered that the *pintadera* was missing soon after they arrived in London.

"Did you leave the bag at any time?" asked one of the policemen.

"No," said Tomás. "It was with me the whole time."

"What about on the plane?" asked the policeman. "Was the bag above you? Or under the seat?"

"No," said Tomás. "I held it in my arms."

"Did you fall asleep on the plane?" he asked.

Tomás and the professor looked at each other.

"Yes, we were very tired," explained Professor Toledo. "We got up very early this morning to get to the airport on time."

The policemen thought this was important. They decided that somebody stole the *pintadera* while the men were asleep on the plane.

"Describe this object for us, please, sir," said one of the policemen.

Tomás described the size and the shape of the *pintadera*, and the sun image made of triangles and circles.

"It's very old, and very special for the Canary Islands," he said. "And it's very valuable."

"Who did you sit next to on the plane?" the policeman asked.

Tomás tried to remember. "It was a girl. She was quite young – maybe about 20," he said. "She had dark hair and a red bag."

"OK," said the policeman. "We have to find this woman. Then I think we'll find your *pintadera*."

Carlota finally arrived at her sister's house and María was very pleased to see her. The beautiful baby was asleep. Carlota wanted to wake her up and play with her. The two sisters talked for a long time about life in Gran Canaria and London. María was very tired. She didn't get much sleep at night because of the baby, but she was very happy with her sweet daughter.

Soon, baby Claudia woke up and the two sisters went for a walk. María pushed the big **pram** down the long street towards the park. There was no more rain, and the sun was starting to shine. Carlota loved being with her sister. She realised how much she missed her.

They reached a **pedestrian crossing** and waited for the green light to cross the road. Lots of cars were driving along the road in front of them. A dirty old car approached them slowly. The car stopped in front of the sisters and a young man got out. His face was pale and Carlota could see that he was carrying a knife! Carlota wanted to scream but she didn't want to frighten María and the baby.

"Give me your bag!" said the man, in an aggressive voice. María looked at him and also saw the knife. Carlota put her hand to her mouth in shock.

"Give me your bag, *now*!" shouted the man. Then, he saw Carlota's red bag on the pram. He **grabbed** it quickly. The sisters were so surprised, they didn't try to stop him. The attacker ran back to the car, and drove away quickly.

María started to cry. Then, baby Claudia started to cry too. Carlota was too surprised to cry. She was also very angry with herself. "Why did I leave my bag on the pram?" she thought. "That was really stupid of me. Why didn't I carry it, like I usually do?"

"You were tired and not thinking clearly. But are you OK?" asked her sister, giving Carlota a **hug**. "At least he didn't hurt us, or the baby."

María started to take Claudia from the pram.

"Hey, what's this?" she said, suddenly. She showed her sister a small brown object. "It looks like ... a *pintadera*. I remember making these at school in Gran Canaria."

"Why was it in Claudia's pram?" asked Carlota, confused.

“I don’t know,” said María. “Maybe it fell from your bag when that man took it.”

“Really?” said Carlota. “But what was it doing there? I never saw it before in my life. Why was it in my bag? Who put it there?”

“I don’t know, it’s a mystery,” said María. "I’m really sorry, Carlota. What a horrible start to your holiday in London!"

The sisters were so surprised, they didn’t try to stop him.

CHAPTERS 3-4 ACTIVITIES

1 The verbs in bold are in the wrong sentences. Write each verb next to the correct sentence.

1. I can hear you. Please don't **hit**. ....
2. Tennis players must **carry** the ball over the net. ....
3. She's very sensitive. It's easy to **shout** her feelings. ....
4. New experiences **hurt** some people. ....
5. It's always a good idea to **shine** extra clothes on a plane.

   ....
6. The sun doesn't **frighten** on a rainy day. ....

2 Choose the correct word to complete each sentence.

1. It is often difficult for **proud** / **elderly** people to walk in the snow.
2. She was **pale** / **pleased** because she didn't feel well.
3. The **suitcase** / **corner** is very heavy. Let me help you with it.
4. This is my stop, so I'm **getting off** / **falling asleep**.
5. They **reached** / **screamed** the end of the path and turned back.

Did you know?

Heathrow Airport in London is one of the busiest airports in the world, with 67 million passengers passing through it a year. Heathrow has got 76,000 workers and there are 1,400 flights a day – that's one every 45 seconds. There is a special terminal on the south side of the airport for important people like royalty, celebrities and heads of state.

3 **The words in bold are mistakes. Write the correct word after each sentence.**

1. **An elderly woman** tried to get on the bus. ....
2. The two men were waiting for a woman with a **yellow** bag.
   ....
3. When the men saw Carlota, she was holding **a phone**.
   ....
4. Carlota left her bag **at María's flat**. ....
5. The man threatened Carlota with a knife because he wanted **her money**. ....
6. **Carlota** found the *pintadera* in Claudia's pram. ....

4 **The author uses suspense to keep the reader interested. One method is if the reader knows something that the character doesn't know. The reader can guess what is going to happen, but can't save the character from danger. What information does the reader know before Carlota in Chapter 3?**

....

....

....

5 **Answer the questions. Write the answers in your notebook.**

1. What observation did Carlota make when she got on the bus?
2. How was Julio connected to the two men?
3. What prevented George and Gary from approaching Carlota when she got off the first bus?
4. Why was Professor Toledo angry with Tomás?
5. What did the police think happened to the *pintadera*?

CHAPTER 5

A New Plan

Gary stopped the car in a car park not far away.

"Well, that was easy," George said. "Now let's have a look at our treasure." He opened the bag and put his hand inside. The bag was full of things, and quite heavy. But there was no *pintadera* inside.

"It's not here," he said.

"It must be," said Gary. "Maybe Julio hid it somewhere. Look for a secret pocket – a special place with a **zip**?"

"No. There isn't anything," said George. "I'm telling you, it's not here."

"Give it to me!" shouted Gary. He took the bag and **turned** it **upside down**. Carlota's things fell onto the floor of the car. There was her **purse**, her sunglasses and some keys. "How much **stuff** has she got here?" Gary said, looking through everything very carefully. There was some chewing gum, two pens and some tissues – but no Canarian treasure.

Gary took the bag and turned it upside down.

Gary was furious. He started the car and quickly returned to the pedestrian crossing to find Carlota, but she wasn't there.

"What are we going to do?" asked George. "If we can't find her, we're not going to get the *pintadera* and we won't get our money!"

"Shut up!" said Gary. "Just keep looking. We'll drive around all night until we see her again, and then I'll kill her!"

George didn't believe that Gary was going to kill the Spanish girl, but he was scared that he could hurt her. George didn't like violence. It was OK to take a bag and disappear. But violence was different. What was going to happen now? He didn't know and he was scared. Gary's face was red and he was driving too fast.

George kept looking for Carlota, but he didn't believe they were going to find her. Gary was driving badly and he didn't stop for red lights. "I hope the police don't arrest us because of Gary's dangerous driving," he thought.

"She can't be far!" said Gary, quietly. "And when I find her ..."

George tried to calm his friend down. Then, he had an idea.

"Gary," he said. "Did you say those historians were going to take the *pintadera* to a museum?"

"Yes. There's going to be an exhibition of *pintaderas* at the British Museum. There are other *pintaderas* in the museum already, but this one is the oldest and the most important."

"Well, why don't we try to take a different one from the museum?" asked George.

"It's impossible," said Gary. "The *pintaderas* in the museum are all locked in **display cases**. We can't steal them."

"It's strange that this old *pintadera* isn't already in the museum," George said. "Why isn't it safely locked in a glass case, like all the others?"

Gary lit a cigarette before he spoke again.

"According to Julio, the Canarian Government wasn't happy that it was leaving the country. They made a copy of it to display at home. It took a long time, and they've only just finished. That's the reason the historians were bringing it now."

Suddenly, Gary stopped the car. "I have got an idea!" he said. "That girl has got the *pintadera*, but what will she do with it? Maybe she'll understand its value, and take it to the museum. It's closed now, but we'll go there and wait for her first thing tomorrow. I'm certain she'll bring it and we'll take it from her before she gives it to the museum."

He started the car again.

"So, what now?" asked George.

"We can't do anything today. But we'll wait all day tomorrow near the museum," said Gary. "She'll go there – I'm certain about that. And we'll finally get it from her. Believe me."

CHAPTER 6

At the Police Station

Professor Manuel Toledo was busy making phone calls to the university and the Canarian Government.

"Yes, somebody stole it," he said. "They took it from us on the plane ... No, they didn't hurt us ... Well, actually, my assistant was carrying it."

Tomás wanted to disappear – this was a catastrophe and he was totally responsible for it. He felt terribly **guilty**. "Now I'll lose my job as the professor's assistant, and I'll never become a professor," he thought.

He remembered his phone call to the organiser of the exhibition at the British Museum. "We advertised your *pintadera* as our main attraction," the organiser told Tomás. "Without it, the exhibition won't be a success."

Tomás understood the consequences of this. "The exhibition will be a **failure** now, and people won't donate money to the university," he thought. "I won't have sufficient money to continue most of my projects on the Canary Islands."

Professor Toledo sat down and drank some tea. "We'll have to make an official report at the police station. The airport police told us that," he said. "I know you feel guilty, Tomás, but we're both responsible. We got up very early this morning to collect the *pintadera* and get to the airport. It's not surprising that we fell asleep on the plane."

Tomás **was relieved** to hear this. "Thanks," he said. "Let's hope the police can help us."

After the incident with the bag, the sisters went to a café to relax. They sat at the back and baby Claudia fell asleep in her pram. Carlota called a number and cancelled her credit cards. "At least, he didn't get my phone. It was in my pocket," Carlota said. "My whole life is in my phone!"

"Yes, that was lucky," said María. "But are you sure you're OK?"

"I'm fine. Don't worry," said Carlota. Really, Carlota was very frightened about the attack, but she was trying to be brave.

"Don't think that London is a dangerous place," said María. "I've lived here for years and nobody has ever attacked me before."

"We were just unlucky," said Carlota. "I was stupid to leave my bag on the pram. Next time, I'll be more careful."

"Are you sure you're OK?" asked María.

"We should tell the police about this," said María.

"OK," said Carlota. "Let's have a coffee and calm down, and then we'll go to the police. How did this thing get into my bag?" she asked, looking at the *pintadera*.

"I don't know," said María. "It's very strange, but I think I recognise it. I saw a picture in the newspaper of a very old *pintadera*. It was going to be in an exhibition at the British Museum. It looked like that."

"Maybe it's valuable," said Carlota. "Let's go and show it to the police. They'll know what to do."

Twenty minutes later, the sisters were explaining their story to a policewoman at the station.

"What was in your bag?" she asked.

"My purse, credit cards, keys, sunglasses," said Carlota. "Fortunately, my phone and my passport weren't in my bag."

"Don't worry," said the policewoman. "But you must cancel your credit cards, so nobody can use them."

"Yes, I did that. But there's something else," Carlota added. "We found this strange ornament in the pram. It was obviously in my bag and fell from it when the thief took it." The woman looked at the *pintadera* curiously. Then her face changed and she stood up. "One moment please," she said and left the room with it.

Five minutes later, a policeman came in and shook their hands.

"Hello," he said. "I'm Detective Martin. Please tell me everything you can about the **theft** of your handbag."

Carlota repeated everything and the detective wrote down all the information.

"Now, please meet some people," he said, and spoke into his phone. A minute later, the policewoman came in with two men.

"This is Professor Manuel Toledo and Mr Tomás Silva," the detective said. "Have you seen these men before?"

Carlota looked closely at their faces. She wasn't sure, but she thought they looked familiar.

"I recognise you!" cried the professor. "You were on our plane! You stole the *pintadera*!" He looked very angry. Carlota did not understand what he was talking about. The other man looked embarrassed.

"I didn't steal anything!" said Carlota, angry. "I'm not a thief! A man with a knife stole my bag. I came here to tell the police about it."

"Are you talking about this object?" the detective asked the professor, showing him the *pintadera*.

The two men **gasped with relief**. "Yes! That's it!" shouted Professor Toledo. "That's our *pintadera*! This girl sat next to Tomás on the plane and she stole it from him while he was asleep!"

Carlota's face went white. "I'm not a thief!" she repeated. "I **swear** I didn't take that thing. You must believe me!"

"Calm down!" Detective Martin said. Then, he spoke in a softer voice. "I believe you, Carlota," he said. "Now listen to me very carefully."

"I recognise you!" cried the professor. "You were on our plane!"

CHAPTERS 5-6 ACTIVITIES

1 Complete the puzzle. Use the clues below.

Across ➤

1. vanish
4. a synonym for *frightened*
5. A hero is … .
6. unfortunate

Down ▼

2. a place in your clothes for keeping things
3. It's … to cross the road when the light is red.

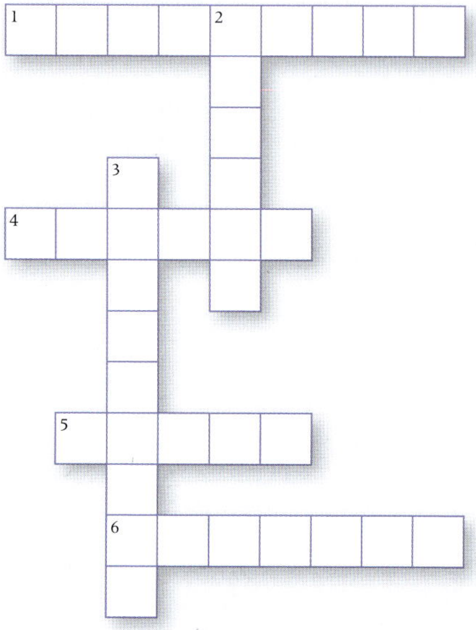

2 Complete the sentences with the words below.

shook their hands *hid* *locked* *kill* *collecting* *success*

1. The thieves .... the money under the floor.
2. I can't get into the room because the door is ....
3. Some wild animals .... to survive.
4. I met our new neighbours and ....
5. She loves .... shells on the sea shore.
6. Your .... usually depends on how hard you work.

Did you know?

Every day, thieves steal over 300 mobile phones in London, most of them on the Underground. The British Transport Police run a programme called Operation Magnum. In Operation Magnum, officers wearing normal clothes travel on the Underground to identify and arrest the thieves.

3 Match A to B to make true sentences about the story.

A

1. Gary returned to the pedestrian crossing
2. George didn't want
3. The Canarian Government made a copy of the *pintadera*
4. Professor Toledo explained the situation
5. Tomás felt terrible because
6. The two sisters went to a coffee shop

B

.... a. he was carrying the *pintadera*.

.... b. to the university and the Canarian Government.

.... c. to relax after the incident.

.... d. to use violence.

.... e. to find Carlota.

.... f. to display in the Canary Islands.

4 Answer the questions. Write the answers in your notebook.

1. Why was Gary furious when George didn't find the *pintadera*?
2. How did Gary and George differ in character?
3. How did Gary plan to get the *pintadera* from the woman?
4. How did Tomás feel about the disappearance of the *pintadera*?
5. What did the Professor say to make Tomás feel better?
6. How did Carlota feel when the professor shouted at her?

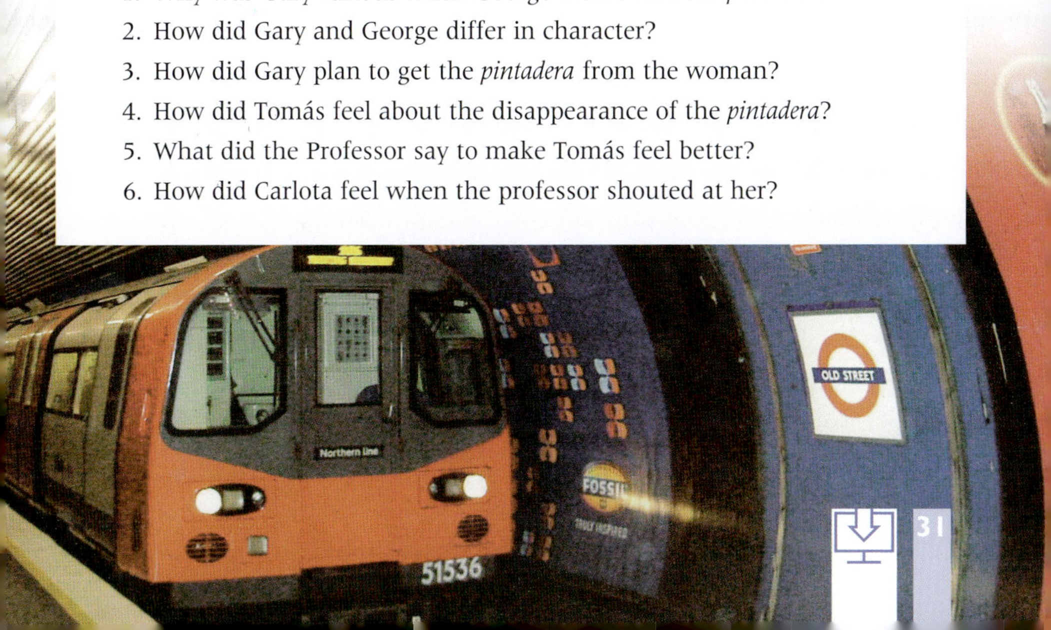

CHAPTER 7

Detective Martin's Plan

Detective Martin specialised in catching international **smuggling rings**. He explained his work to the four of them. Many criminals worked at airports and tried to send out their different goods illegally – goods like drugs, **valuables** and sometimes, ancient artefacts. "It's a challenge to steal something important and then get it to another country," he explained. "The best way is to hide the object in an innocent passenger's bag. That person will take it into the country for them, usually without knowing it. Then, the passenger leaves the airport with the smuggled object and the criminals are waiting to take it from them. We see it again and again."

"So, somebody put our *pintadera* into this young woman's bag?" asked Tomás.

"Yes. I'm certain of it," said the detective. "It was probably the same person. First, they stole it from you, and then, they put it in Carlota's bag. Tell me, at the airport, did you leave your bag unsupervised at any time?"

"So, somebody put our pintadera *into this young woman's bag?" asked Tomás.*

"No, of course not," said Professor Toledo. "We're not stupid! There are constant announcements over the **loudspeaker**, **warning** passengers not to leave their bags unsupervised."

Then he looked at his assistant with a question in his eyes.

"No, my bag was with me all the time," said Tomás. "I was carrying it on my shoulder – except in the duty free. I put it in the trolley with my jacket because I was hot. But the trolley was with me all the time."

"Hmm," said the detective. "It's not difficult to take something from a trolley, especially with lots of people around."

Then he looked at Carlota.

"How about you, Carlota? Did you leave your bag at all – even for a minute?" Carlota was looking very uncomfortable. She told the detective about the good-looking man in the coffee shop. "He offered to watch my bag for me while I checked my flight times," she said. "But it was less than a minute."

"That's all he needed to put it inside your bag," said the detective.

"He said they were delaying my plane, but they weren't," said Carlota. She felt very foolish now. "It was just an excuse to make me go and check, and leave my bag. He **tricked** me very easily. I was really stupid," she said.

"No, you weren't," said the detective. "These guys are professionals. They trick people every day, and they always work together. At least, we've got the *pintadera*. This time, those criminals didn't win!"

"That's true," said Professor Toledo. "We should take it straight to the museum. It will be safe there and ready for the start of the exhibition tomorrow."

"We'll do that," said Detective Martin. "But first, we need to catch those criminals."

"How do we do that?" asked Tomás.

"Well, we need a detailed description of the thief from these two young ladies. Then, we can make a sketch, and give it to all our officers," said Detective Martin.

"And then what?" asked Professor Toledo.

"They know that Carlota has got the *pintadera*, and she could take it to the British Museum – especially as they're having a big exhibition of these things. I think they'll wait for you there to take it from you before you give it to the museum. But we'll get them first." He looked at Carlota. "Will you go there tomorrow morning, with the *pintadera* very clearly in your hand?"

"*And then what?*" demanded María. "They'll attack my sister again? Is that what you want? They had a knife last time! Next time, they could have a gun! It's too dangerous! She's my responsibility and she's not going!"

"Don't worry," Detective Martin **assured** her. "There will be police officers all over the museum to keep Carlota safe and there are security cameras everywhere."

Carlota felt afraid, but she wanted to help the police catch the criminals. "I'll do it," she said, timidly. "But stay near me!"

Everybody agreed that Carlota was very brave.

CHAPTER 8

Inside the British Museum

Outside the British Museum, a colourful poster was blowing in the wind. The poster was advertising a new exhibition of ancient art from the Canary Islands. The museum was still closed because it was early in the morning. In a car parked across the street, Gary and George were waiting for Carlota.

Finally, people began to appear on the street. Some people were on their way to work, carrying briefcases and mobile phones. George looked around nervously. He was still scared that Gary was going to hurt the Spanish girl. Gary was angrier than usual because he was not accustomed to getting up early.

"I'm hungry," George said. "Let's get some food. It'll just take a minute. The museum's not open yet."

"No. We can't leave the car," said Gary. "Maybe she'll come early. This is our only opportunity to get the *pintadera* and make a lot of money."

"OK. So, I'll go," said George. "You stay here."

"No," Gary said. "I'll go. But don't close your eyes for one second!" he shouted, before he got out of the car. Then he gave George the knife. "Take this," he said. "She'll see that and give you the *pintadera* immediately. OK?"

George said nothing as Gary left the car. He put the knife under the seat. He wasn't going to use it. He was tired and just wanted to go home and forget the whole idea.

Somebody opened the doors of the museum, and some tourists started to arrive. George watched them entering the museum. Was the Spanish girl in that crowd? More visitors were arriving from all directions.

Then he saw her – for just a second, but then he lost her in the crowd. Where did she go? There! It was her! This time, he was certain.

George got out of the car and closed the door. He thought about taking Gary's knife for one second, but he knew he wasn't going to use it on an innocent girl, so he left it in the car. Slowly, George started to walk towards the museum entrance. He was very nervous.

Then he saw her – for just a second, but then he lost her in the crowd.

George had mixed feelings. The Spanish girl had the treasure with her, that was certain. He wanted to sell that *pintadera* and become rich. But he didn't want to hurt her. "Should I **pretend** I haven't seen her?" he thought. "But then, what will I tell Gary? He's dangerous and violent and I'm afraid of him. Gary thought it was going to be very easy to get the *pintadera*, but so far, it's been very difficult."

Then, he saw the girl again.

George followed Carlota around the museum, keeping a distance between them. He was worried she could remember his face. The museum was very big and there were a lot of interesting things to look at. A woman with a microphone was talking to a small group of people.

"Hello, everybody," she said. "We've got some special things for you to see today!" The people in the crowd were listening carefully. The woman continued talking.

"Has anybody here been to the Canary Islands?" she asked. Some people raised their hands.

"Well, did you know that the islands were not always Spanish? Native people lived on the islands before the Spanish came, and we can learn a lot about them from things they left behind." George stopped to listen to the woman.

"The native population had many small decorations, called *pintaderas*," she said. "These were usually made of **clay**, and had

designs on them – sometimes circles, sometimes triangles. The people put them in high places as ornaments. Look, here are pictures of *pintaderas*." George looked at the pictures curiously. "Oh, that's how they look," he thought. "It's incredible that those simple ornaments are very valuable."

Then he heard a voice in his ear.

"Where's the girl?" asked Gary. "I saw the car was empty, so I realised you were in here. I can't see her anywhere."

"She's over there," said George, pointing to the group of people. Then he realised he had no idea where she was! He couldn't see her!

"*Where*?" **whispered** Gary, angry. George could feel something in his back. Gary was holding a gun!

"If you've lost her, I'll kill you!" said Gary. George was afraid.

"She was here a minute ago," said George. "She must be nearby. Don't worry, we'll find her."

Gary put the gun into his pocket. "Let's separate," he said. "That way, we can find her more quickly. If you see her, make sure you get that *pintadera*. Don't **fail** me!"

"OK," said George. Gary walked in one direction and George walked in the other. He wanted to find Carlota before Gary did.

"She's over there," said George, pointing to the group of people.

CHAPTERS 7-8 ACTIVITIES

1 Tick (✓) the correct picture to match each word.

1. agree

a ☐ 

b ☐ 

2. afraid

a ☐ 

b ☐ 

3. good-looking

a ☐ 

b ☐ 

4. empty

a ☐ 

b ☐ 

2 Complete the words according to the definitions. Then write the letters in the squares on the lines below to complete the name of the first people to inhabit the Canary Islands.

1. You shoot with this. .... [........]₁ n
2. The media does this to sell something. [........]₂ .... v .... t .... s ....
3. a picture or pattern on an item d .... s .... [........]₃
4. A difficult problem is a … . [........]₄ [........]₅ a l l .... n g ....
5. a kind of bag for important documents b .... [........]₆ .... s ....
6. another word for *products* .... o .... [........]₇

The G ....₁ ....₂ ....₃ ....₄ ....₅ ....₆ ....₇ were the first people to inhabit the Canary Islands.

3 Complete the sentences with the correct name.

George *Gary* *Carlota* *María* *Detective Martin* *Professor Toledo*

1. .... specialised in catching criminals.
2. .... felt very stupid.
3. .... wanted to take the *pintadera* to the museum immediately.
4. .... didn't want to let Carlota help the police.
5. .... didn't want to continue with the plan to steal the *pintadera*.
6. .... was ready to use a gun, so he could get the *pintadera*.

4 The protagonist is the main character in the story. He / She is often given a challenge in the story. Answer the following questions.

1. Who is the protagonist in the story?

   ....

2. What challenge is she given?

   ....

5 Answer the questions. Write the answers in your notebook.

1. According to Detective Martin, how did smuggling rings send goods out of the country?
2. What did Carlota realise about the man in the coffee shop?
3. How did Detective Martin plan to catch the criminals?
4. What was George's conflict?
5. Why did Gary threaten George?
6. What was Gary's suggestion for finding Carlota more quickly?

Did you know?

Philip Baron was the leader of one of the biggest smuggling rings in the UK. He smuggled £110 million of illegal drugs into the UK. For five years, 22 UK and international police forces tried to catch Baron's gang. The police finally arrested him in 2011. Baron received an 18-year prison sentence for his crimes.

CHAPTER 9

Playing Cat and Mouse

George walked around the exhibition and saw lots of different *pintaderas*. Some were very beautiful. Trying to look like a museum visitor, he read the information about Canarian history. Two men in suits were standing nearby, talking in Spanish. One was older than the other one. They looked very official, like they worked at the museum, and they were holding a yellow piece of paper. George thought they were looking at him, so he moved away from them and suddenly his heart froze. Two policemen were standing together, also holding yellow pieces of paper. George could see a picture of a man's face on the paper. Now he was terrified. Were they all looking for him? Did the Spanish girl go to the police and identify him?

"I must get out of here now," George thought.

Two policemen were standing together, also holding yellow pieces of paper.

He turned and walked quickly towards the door of the museum, trying to look **casual**. When he got outside, he remembered Gary. George considered going back into the museum, but he was too afraid of the police and the men with the yellow paper. He began to run and didn't look back. He ran and ran until his legs began to hurt.

Gary was still looking for Carlota. He walked all around the museum and was getting worried. "I hope it's not too late to steal the *pintadera*," he thought. "Has she already given it to the museum?"

He entered a room of **swords and armour** from Japan. "This isn't the right place," he thought. "Where on Earth is the Gran Canaria exhibition?"

Then, he turned around and saw the back of Carlota's head. At last! And what did she have in her hand? It looked like – the *pintadera*! This was his opportunity. He ran after Carlota, but suddenly, a big crowd of people surrounded him. He couldn't move quickly. Carlota was just in front of him. She was looking for something. Gary could not move close enough to take the *pintadera* from her.

Finally, he pushed through the crowd, but Carlota wasn't there. He couldn't see her anywhere. He ran down long **corridors**, getting angrier every minute. He entered a room of Indian items and saw a dark-haired woman in a mirror. She turned around – but it wasn't Carlota! He looked down to the other end of the long corridor and there she was! Gary ran after her, determined that this time, he was going to catch her.

Carlota held the *pintadera* **tightly** in her hand. She walked around the museum as fast as she could, following Detective Martin's instructions. When she arrived at one end of the floor, she turned and walked in another direction. She never looked back and she never stopped moving. It was like playing Cat and Mouse.

She saw beautiful items from around the world. Some of them were thousands of years old. She wanted to stop and look at everything in this incredible museum, but it was impossible. She had a very important job to do. She knew they were following her and that she was in danger. Carlota tried not to think about the danger. She just thought about those criminals going to jail. Soon, she must leave the crowd and go somewhere less busy to give the criminals an opportunity to catch her. Then, the police could arrest them. It was all part of their plan. But the plan was a very dangerous one. Was it going to work?

Professor Toledo and Tomás were wearing their best suits for the exhibition. They looked very elegant as they stood and greeted the visitors. Tomás was holding a yellow piece of paper with a drawing of the thief's face.

"What do you think of the exhibition, Tomás?" asked the professor.

"I think it's fascinating," said Tomás. "Everybody is enjoying it."

"Yes," said the professor. "You worked hard organising everything. Well done!"

"Thank you," said Tomás. He was very proud of the exhibition and happy with the professor's **praise**. Tomás watched the people in the crowd, looking at the displays and reading all the information. They seemed very interested in Canarian history. He hoped the exhibition would raise a lot of money for his research.

But one man in the crowd was a little strange. He was looking around for somebody and ignoring the exhibits completely. Tomás checked the picture on the yellow piece of paper. Was it? Yes, maybe it was the same man! Tomás whispered to the professor, but when Professor Toledo tried to see the man, he wasn't there.

Officer Smith also had a picture in his hand. He knew the man's face very well. His instructions were clear: don't arrest the man – just alert the official controlling the security cameras in the building.

"Look! That's him!" said his partner, William Davis. But the man, suddenly, turned around and walked away. Officer Smith reached for his radio.

"We've got him," he said.

CHAPTER 10

All Alone!

Carlota was walking very quickly. She knew that someone was following her. Gary held the gun in his pocket. He was desperate to get the *pintadera* and he wasn't afraid to use the gun in the museum. The only thing he could think about was the money. His money! He didn't know where George was and he didn't care. Maybe it was better alone, without George. Then, Gary could get all the money.

He followed the Spanish girl through lots of different rooms. Each room was full of people and it was difficult to approach her. Then, his luck changed. The girl started to walk towards the toilets! She was going in! This was his chance.

Carlota entered the toilets. Inside, two of the cubicle doors were closed. She knew that police officers were hiding behind them. When the thief came in after her, she wasn't going to be alone.

Gary approached the door. He saw a sign on a drinks machine next to the wall. It said, '**OUT OF ORDER**' in big letters. He took the sign and put it on the door. "Now nobody will enter the toilet," he thought. Then, he opened the door and walked inside. He saw the girl standing in front of the mirror, doing her hair.

Gary opened the door and walked inside.

"What have you got in your hand?" he asked her. Carlota looked at him, pretending to be surprised.

"You can't come in here," she said. "This toilet is for women only."

"I said, *what have you got in your hand!*" shouted Gary.

"Oh this," said Carlota. "It belongs to the museum. I'm just trying to find somebody to give it to."

"You can give it to me," said Gary, walking towards her.

"I don't think so," said Carlota. "It's very old. I think somebody at the museum is waiting for it."

Gary was very close now. Carlota was terrified.

"Give me that thing, now!" Gary screamed, and took his gun from his pocket.

"Help! He's got a gun!" shouted Carlota. She waited for the policemen but nobody came! She ran to the cubicle doors and pushed them open, but they were empty! She was all alone!

"It's just you and me, darling," said Gary. He hit Carlota on the side of her head with his gun. She **fainted** and fell to the floor. When she woke up, Gary wasn't there and the *pintadera* was missing.

The man in the control room was looking at all the television screens. He was controlling the cameras to see all around the museum. He couldn't see Carlota anywhere. He couldn't see the thief either.

"What's happening?" asked Detective Martin.

"I don't know – I've lost them," said the controller. "I was watching the toilet door, but she didn't arrive. The officers are in place in the toilet cubicles inside."

"So, where is she?" said Detective Martin. "I don't like this. Maybe she's in danger."

"I don't understand," said the controller. "They've disappeared."

"How many toilets are there in the museum?" the detective asked.

"There are lots," said a museum official. "It's a big museum. But she knew she must go to the toilets on the third floor. And she hasn't arrived there."

"Maybe she went to the *wrong* toilets!" said the detective. "And that guy is in there with her!"

"I hope not," said the controller. "Wait. Let me move the cameras around the floor." Nobody spoke while the controller was working. Everybody **held their breath**, very scared.

"Wait," said the controller, finally. "There's a toilet on the opposite side of the museum with an 'OUT OF ORDER' sign on it."

"But we checked all the toilets this morning," said the museum official. "None of them were out of order."

"That must be the one!" Detective Martin shouted. "We'll go there immediately. You keep watching the cameras."

"I will," said the controller. "Good luck. I hope we're not too late."

"There's a toilet on the opposite side of the museum with an 'OUT OF ORDER' sign on it," said the controller.

CHAPTERS 9-10 ACTIVITIES

1 Match each word in A to the correct definition in B.

A

1. froze
2. alone
3. greeted
4. chance
5. determined
6. jail
7. surrounded

B

.... a. opportunity
.... b. said hello, welcomed
.... c. without anybody
.... d. a place for criminals
.... e. circled
.... f. didn't move
.... g. persistent

2 Complete each sentence with a word from Exercise 1.

1. The woman .... her husband with a smile.
2. I'll give you one more .... to answer the question.
3. The police .... the building to try to catch the thief.
4. She went out .... because her friend didn't want to go with her.
5. The guard .... when the thief pointed a gun at him.
6. The student studied all weekend because he was .... to pass the test.
7. The policeman arrested the man and took him to ....

3 Who or what does the word in bold refer to? Choose the correct answer.

1. George thought **they** were looking at him, so he moved away from them.
   a. Tomás and the professor b. Carlota and María c. the police officers
2. George was looking around for **somebody** and ignoring the exhibits completely.
   a. the *pintadera* b. Gary c. Carlota
3. **His** instructions were clear: don't arrest the man.
   a. Officer Smith b. Gary c. the professor
4. Carlota knew that police officers were hiding behind **them**.
   a. Gary and George b. the cubicle doors c. the visitors
5. "I've lost **them**," said the controller.
   a. the cameras b. Gary and George c. Carlota and Gary
6. "That must be the **one**!" Detective Martin shouted.
   a. thief b. *pintadera* c. toilet

4 Answer the questions. Write the answers in your notebook.

1. Why did George leave the museum?
2. How did Tomás identify the strange man?
3. Why was Carlota brave?
4. Why did Carlota think it was safe to enter the toilets?
5. How did Gary try to stop people from entering the toilets?
6. Why didn't the policemen come to help Carlota?

Did you know?

In many museums with valuable items, security officers put sensors around paintings to detect any movements. There are cameras filming the halls all the time and the windows have often got sensors on them to tell if someone breaks the glass.

CHAPTER 11

A Great Story to Tell

Detective Martin and another policeman ran straight to the toilets. They saw the 'OUT OF ORDER' sign on the door. When they opened the door, they saw Carlota lying on the floor. Her head was **bleeding**.

"Carlota! Are you OK? What happened?" Carlota got onto her feet slowly. She felt **dizzy** and confused.

"The thief came in here," she said. "I was alone! The police officers weren't here to protect me."

"I'm very sorry, but you made a terrible mistake," explained Officer Smith. "They were waiting in different toilets at the opposite side of the museum. What happened to your head?"

"He hit me with something hard," said Carlota. "I fainted and he escaped. He took the *pintadera*," she said.

"Don't worry," said Detective Martin. "We'll catch him. I'm just happy you're OK."

"I'm fine," said Carlota. "My head hurts a bit, but I think I'm OK."

"We'll take you to hospital and a doctor will check your head," the detective said. "Have you ever been in a police car with the lights flashing and siren going?"

"Of course not!" Carlota smiled. "I don't think it's necessary, but it'll be a great story to tell my friends back in Gran Canaria!"

"Can you see him?" Detective Martin asked the controller on the radio.

"Yes," said the controller. "He's running towards the exit. Be very careful. He's got a gun."

"A gun!" cried Officer Smith. "This man is more dangerous than we thought. Wait until he gets outside before you arrest him. He mustn't fire his gun in the museum. We don't want to hurt anybody."

"Right," said the controller. "I'll call the officers and they'll meet you outside. Go quickly! He's close to the door. I can't see him when he's outside the museum."

"I'm on my way," said Detective Martin. He ran as fast as he could to the exit door and saw the back of Gary's head as he ran into the street outside.

"Everybody! Get outside!" he shouted into his radio. "He's left the museum. We need to catch him now!"

Officer Smith saw Gary getting into his car. Then, he started the **engine** and drove very quickly down the street. Without thinking, the officer ran into the road and stood in the way of the car.

"Come back!" shouted one of the other officers. "It's too dangerous!" Officer Smith didn't listen. He raised his hand for Gary to stop the car, but Gary didn't stop – or reduce his speed. At the last minute, he tried to drive the car around the policeman, but he lost control. The car hit Officer Smith and knocked him to the ground. Then, the car **crashed into** a parked lorry. A crowd of people ran to see what was happening. The officer tried to stand but his leg was too painful. Was it broken?

"Now it's your turn for the hospital!" said Detective Martin.

He tried to drive the car around the policeman, but he lost control.

Carlota was sitting in the emergency department with a large **bandage** on her head. She was waiting to go home with María and her family.

"I'm very proud of you," said María. "You're the bravest person in the world. Stupid, but very brave!"

"That's not true," said Carlota. She felt embarrassed when people complimented her. "I'm just glad it's all over," she said. "This is certainly my most memorable holiday!"

"Yes, you won't forget this, I'm sure!" said another voice, and everybody laughed. They looked over to a wheelchair next to Carlota, where Officer Smith was sitting, his broken leg **in a plaster cast**.

"Are you going to be OK?" asked Carlota.

"I'll be fine," said the young policeman. "My leg will get better, and I'll be back to work. But I've learnt not to jump in front of cars again!"

"I've learnt not to jump in front of cars again!" said the young policeman.

"What happened to the thief?" asked Carlota.

"Didn't you hear?" said María. "He was **badly injured** in the accident. He's going to be in hospital for a long time, and then he'll go to jail. They pulled him from the car and he was still holding the *pintadera*. It broke into pieces."

"It broke!" exclaimed María's husband. "Oh, no! Then all your work was useless! That *pintadera* was very important and valuable!"

Carlota and Officer Smith smiled at each other. They were happy because they both knew a secret.

CHAPTER 12

A Special Piece of Canarian History

When the doctor finally **released** Carlota from hospital, María and her husband wanted to go home, but Carlota had another idea.

"I want to go back to the museum," she said.

"*The museum?*" said María. "Are you crazy? Why do you want to go there again, after your terrible experience?"

She looked very serious, but Carlota was smiling.

"I want to go and see the Canarian exhibition properly," said Carlota. "And all the other interesting exhibits. I couldn't concentrate on anything last time because I was only thinking about one thing – staying alive! But come with me, there's something you must see."

María's husband drove them back to the museum and Carlota was very excited about her surprise.

Inside the museum, there was another big crowd, but this time they were all standing around a platform with a new display case. Two strong security guards were standing next to the platform, with two men in suits. Carlota and María recognised these men as Professor Toledo and Tomás Silva.

In the centre of the platform was a glass box, with a very special item in it.

"Wait," said María, pointing at the box. "Isn't that the ... ?"

Carlota didn't say anything. She let Tomás Silva explain everything to the crowd.

"You are looking at a very special piece of Canarian history," he said. "This *pintadera* is very old. It is the oldest example we have in our collection. This *pintadera* teaches us a lot about the Aboriginal people of the Canary Islands. But that is not the only reason it is special. We nearly lost this piece of history forever. A **gang** of criminals tried to steal this artefact from us because they knew it was very valuable. Yesterday, they almost succeeded."

The crowd looked shocked, and started to whisper to each other.

"The British Museum has got **fake** copies of our *pintadera*, as this is usually on display in Gran Canaria," Tomás continued. "With the help of the police and the museum, we used one of these fake copies to catch the thief, and it broke into pieces. Luckily, the real *pintadera* was safe in the museum and for that reason, we can share it with you all today." There was a round of applause from the crowd.

"I don't believe it," whispered María. "Did you know that you were walking around the museum with a fake *pintadera*?"

"Of course I did!" said Carlota. "It was Detective Martin's idea. He wasn't going to take a risk with the real thing! Now, let's visit the exhibition properly."

The sisters enjoyed the exhibition and learnt a lot about their island's history. After a while, they met Tomás Silva. He was looking very happy.

"Congratulations, Mr Silva," said Carlota. "You organised a very interesting exhibition."

"Thank you so much," he said. "I'm very pleased you like it. Can you see that man over there?" he asked, and he pointed to a large man with wild grey hair. "He's a museum owner from the United States. He's very rich. He really likes the exhibition, and he's agreed to give us enough money to continue excavating on the Canary Islands for another five years!"

"Congratulations!" cried Carlota.

"And the best thing is, at the end of the five years, I'll be a **full-time** professor," said Tomás. "Professor Toledo has just confirmed it."

"Well done," said María. "I think you **deserve** it."

Then she spoke to Carlota. "Come on," she said. "I've had enough excitement for one day!"

"I agree," said Carlota. "I think it's time we went back to your house. I want to start to plan my holiday and all the things we must visit in London."

The two sisters walked out of the museum, pushing the sleeping baby Claudia in front of them. Their dangerous adventure was now behind them.

"Come on," María said. "I've had enough excitement for one day!"

CHAPTERS 11-12 ACTIVITIES

1 Complete the sentences with the words on Officer Smith's cast.

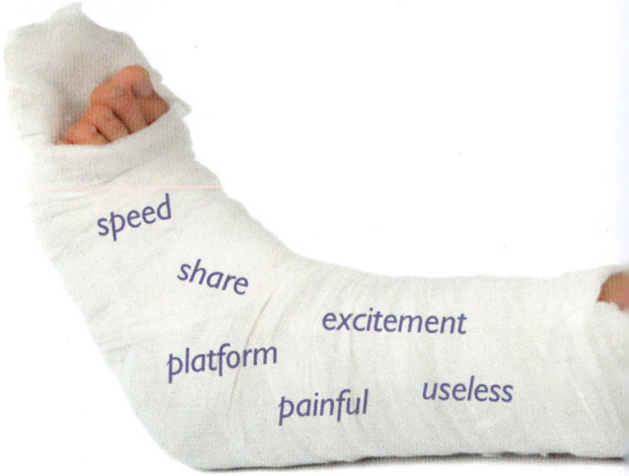

1. I want to .... some information with you.
2. The answer is no. It's .... to argue with me.
3. You are driving at a high .... Please slow down!
4. I hurt my leg. It's very .... to walk on it.
5. There was a lot of .... when the famous painting arrived.
6. The visitors stood on the .... , next to the display case.

2 Complete the police report with the words and phrases below.

lying broken alive succeeded take a risk knocked

POLICE REPORT

CASE NO. A4-761532 **DATE:** 26th August

REPORTING OFFICER: Officer Smith **PREPARED BY:** Detective Martin

SUMMARY OF EVENT:

The thief decided to 1. .... and follow the woman into the ladies' toilets. He hit her on the head with a gun and 2. .... her to the ground. Her head was bleeding, but she was 3. .... When I entered the toilets, I found the victim 4. .... on the floor. Her arms and legs weren't 5. ...., but she had a minor head injury. I sent the other officers to look for the thief. In the end, they 6. .... in catching him.

3 The plot is the sequence of events that make up a story. Number the events in the correct order according to the plot of the story.

.... a. Detective Martin ran to the exit to catch Gary.

.... b. The two sisters left the museum with Claudia.

.... c. Gary's car hit Officer Smith and knocked him to the ground.

.... d. Detective Martin ran to the toilets.

.... e. Carlota showed María the real *pintadera* in the museum.

.... f. Officer Smith and Carlota were sitting in the emergency department.

4 Answer the questions. Write the answers in your notebook.

1. Who found Carlota in the toilets?
2. What instructions did Officer Smith give the controller?
3. Why did Officer Smith run into the road?
4. Why did María think Carlota was crazy?
5. What was Carlota and Officer Smith's secret?
6. How do we know that Tomás was successful in his mission?

Did you know?

In 1985, thieves stole 140 very valuable artefacts from the National Museum of Anthropology in Mexico. It was Christmas Eve and the holiday celebrations distracted the guards. One of the artefacts was a vase in the shape of a monkey, worth more than $20 million!

GLOSSARY

English	Castellano	Català
assured	aseguró	va assegurar
badly injured	gravemente herido	greument ferit
bandage	venda	bena
banged on	aporrearon	van copejar
bargain	ganga; de ocasión	ganga; d'ocasió
bleeding	sangrando	sagnant
casual	despreocupado, tranquilo	despreocupat, tranquil
clay	arcilla	argila
corridors	pasillos	passadissos
counter	mostrador	taulell
crashed into	se chocó / estrelló contra	va topar / es va estavellar contra
crowd	gente; multitud; público	gent; multitud; públic
deep in	enfrascado en	immers en
deserve	mereces	mereixes
display cases	vitrinas	vitrines
disturb	molestar	molestar
dizzy	mareada	marejada
embarrassed	avergonzada	avergonyida
engine	motor	motor
fail	falles	fallis
failure	fracaso	fracàs
fainted	se desmayó	es va desmaiar
fake	falsas	falses
full-time	titular	titular
funds	fondos	fons
gang	banda	banda

English	Euskara	Galego
assured	ziurtatu zion	asegurou
badly injured	larriki zauritu	gravemente ferido
bandage	hesgailu	vendaxe
banged on	joka hasi ziren	abatanaron, golpearon
bargain	mauka; aukerako	ganga; de ocasión
bleeding	odoletan	sangrando, a sangrar
casual	arduragabe, lasai	despreocupado, tranquilo
clay	buztin	arxila
corridors	korridore(ak)	corredores
counter	salmahai	mostrador
crashed into	-en kontra jo zuen	bateu / esnaquizouse contra
crowd	jendetza; mordo; jende	xente; multitude; público
deep in	-n murgildua	enfrascado en
deserve	merezi duzu	mereces
display cases	beira-arasa(k)	vitrinas
disturb	molestatzea	molestar, amolar
dizzy	zorabiatuta, ondoezik	mareada
embarrassed	lotsatuta	avergoñada
engine	motor	motor
fail	huts egin	erres
failure	porrot	fracaso
fainted	zorabiatu egin zen	desmaiouse
fake	faltsu	falsas
full-time	titular	titular
funds	funts(ak)	fondos
gang	gaizkile-talde	banda

GLOSSARY

English	Castellano	Català
gasped with relief	dieron un grito ahogado de alivio	van fer un crit ofegat d'alleujament
grabbed	agarró, cogió	va agafar
guilty	culpable	culpable
held their breath	contuvieron la respiración	va contenir la respiració
hug	abrazo	abraçada
in a plaster cast	escayolada	enguixada
leather	cuero, piel	cuir, pell
loudspeaker	altavoz	altaveu
miss	perder(se); echaba de menos	perdre('s); enyorava
out of order	(de) averiado	(de) fora de servei
pedestrian crossing	paso de peatones / cebra	pas de vianants / zebra
praise	elogios, alabanzas	elogis, lloances
pram	cochecito (de niño)	cotxet
pretend	fingir	fingir
property developer	promotor inmobiliario	promotor immobiliari
purse	monedero	portamonedes
queue	cola	cua
raise	recaudar; levantaron	recaptar; van aixecar
released	dio el alta a	va donar l'alta a
reluctantly	a regañadientes, de mala gana	a contracor, de mala gana
research	investigación	investigació
smuggling rings	redes de contrabando	xarxes de contraban
stuff	cosas	coses
swear	juro	juro

English	Euskara	Galego
gasped with relief	lasaitasun-oihu ito bat egin zuten	deron un berro afogado de alivio
grabbed	hartu zuen	agarrou, colleu
guilty	errudun	culpábel
held their breath	arnasari eutsi zioten	contiveron o alento
hug	besarkada	aperta
in a plaster cast	igeltsutan	escaiolada
leather	larru	coiro, pel
loudspeaker	bozgorailu	altofalante
miss	(aukera) galdu	perder(se); facía de menos
out of order	matxuratuta	(de) avariado
pedestrian crossing	oinezkoen pasabide	paso de peóns / cebra
praise	gorespen(ak), laudorio(ak)	eloxios, gabanzas
pram	haur-kotxe	carriño (de neno)
pretend	plantak egin	finxir
property developer	higiezinen sustatzaile	promotor inmobiliario
purse	diru-zorro	moedeiro
queue	ilara	cola
raise	bildu; jaso zituzten	recadar; ergueron
released	alta eman zion	deulle a alta a
reluctantly	gogoz kontra	de mal grado, de mala gana
research	ikerketa	pescuda
smuggling rings	kontrabando-sare(ak)	redes de contrabando
stuff	gauza	cousas
swear	zin egiten dut	xuro

GLOSSARY

English	Castellano	Català
swords and armour	espadas y armaduras	espases i armadures
theft	robo	robatori
tightly	con fuerza	amb força
tricked	engañó (a)	va enganyar
trolley	carro	carretó
turned … upside down	puso boca abajo	va posar boca avall
valuables	objetos de valor	objectes de valor
warning	advirtiendo / avisando a	advertint / avisant
was relieved	le tranquilizó	el va tranquil·litzar
waste	perder	perdre
whispered	susurró	va xiuxiuejar
wrapped	envuelto	embolicat
zip	cremallera	cremallera

GLOSSARY

English	Euskara	Galego
swords and armour	ezpata(k) eta armadura(k)	espadas e armaduras
theft	lapurreta	roubo
tightly	estuki	con forza
tricked	engainatu ninduen	enganou (a)
trolley	orga	carro
turned … upside down	buruz behera jarri zuen	puxo boca abaixo
valuables	objektu baliotsu(ak)	obxectos de valor
warning	ohartarazten	advertindo / avisando a
was relieved	lasaitu egin zen	tranquilizouno
waste	galdu	perder
whispered	xuxurlatu zuen	moumeou
wrapped	bilduta	envolto
zip	kremailera	cremalleira

CROSS-CURRICULAR FOCUS
The Canary Islands

GEOGRAPHY

One hundred kilometres from the southern **border** of Morocco **lie** the Canary Islands – a group of 13 islands created by volcanic activity. These islands are part of Spain. The seven main islands are Tenerife, Fuerteventura, Gran Canaria, Lanzarote, La Palma, La Gomera and El Hierro.

Many tourists visit the Canary Islands because of their beautiful beaches and subtropical climate. They like hiking in the mountains, especially the Pico de Teide on Tenerife. This is the highest mountain at 3,718 metres above sea level.

Each island has got its own climate, depending on its location. The islands closer to the African coast are more like a desert. Those on the western side of the archipelago are greener. Tenerife and Gran Canaria have got the best of both worlds. The northern part of the island is green because the wet wind coming from the Atlantic Ocean influences the climate. But if you go to the southern part of the island, it is dry.

The inhabitants of the Canary Islands earn money from farming, fishing and industry, but they live mainly from tourism. The most important tourist islands are Tenerife, Gran Canaria, Lanzarote and Fuerteventura.

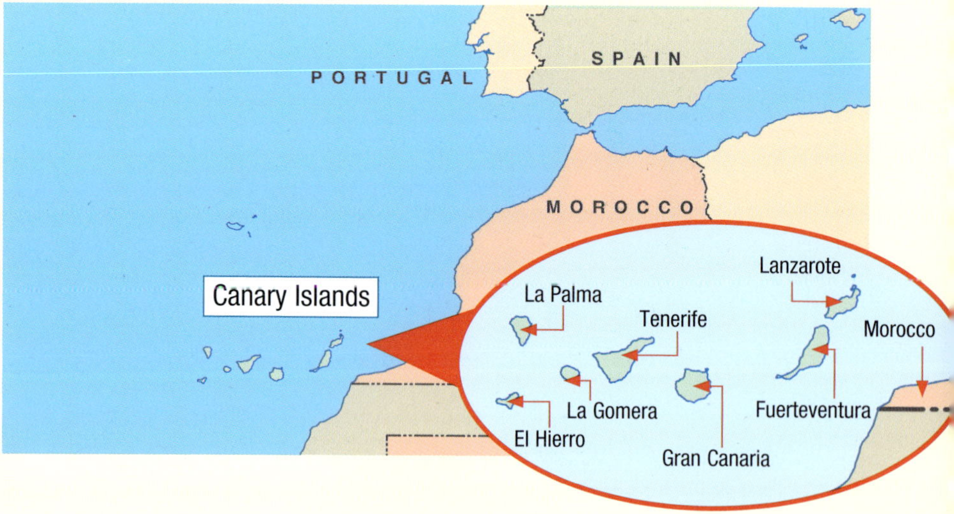

border	frontera	frontera	muga	fronteira
lie	se encuentran	estan situades a	daude	atópanse

1 Are the sentences true (T) or false (F)? Circle the correct letter. Then write the circled letters to complete the sentence below.

	T	F
1. Volcanic eruptions formed the Canary Islands.	c	w
2. Tourists like the Canaries because of their climate.	o	e
3. The highest mountain is on El Hierro.	d	t
4. The islands near the African coast are wet.	e	l
5. Tenerife has got a mixed climate.	a	n
6. The islanders depend only on tourism to earn money.	i	n

Tenerife has got the same flag as S .... d.

2 Answer the questions.

1. Where are the Canary Islands?

....

2. Which country are the Canary Islands part of?

....

3. How many islands are there in the Canary Islands archipelago?

....

4. What is one of the main attractions on Tenerife?

....

5. Why is Tenerife green in the north?

....

6. Which are the most important tourist islands?

....

HISTORY

Who first discovered the Canary Islands? Nobody really knows, but it's possible the original inhabitants came from the north of Africa around 1,000 BC or earlier. They were called Guanches. Ancient artefacts tell us about the lives of the Guanches. One of these artefacts is a kind of stamp called a *pintadera*. The Guanches made these stamps from fired clay and decorated them with geometric shapes. Today, you can see *pintaderas* in museums. Most of them come from archeological sites in Gran Canaria and Tenerife. We don't know what their purpose was. One theory is that the natives used them to put natural **dyes** on their body for decoration.

After the fall of the Greek and Roman Empires, people forgot about the Canaries. The Guanches lived there peacefully until 1402. Then, Spanish conquerors arrived on the islands and slowly, Spain took control of all the islands, conquering the last island, Tenerife.

The Canary Islands became an important location on the **trade** route between Europe and the Americas. In later centuries, several nations tried to attack the Canaries, but they didn't succeed and the islands are still a part of Spain to this day.

Statue of a Guanche

dyes	tintes	tints	tindu(ak)	tinguiduras
trade	comercial	comercial	merkataritza-	comercial

3 Match A to B to make true sentences about the text.

A

1. The first inhabitants
2. Many *pintaderas*
3. Today, people
4. The Spanish
5. The islands

B

.... a. aren't sure what the *pintaderas* were used for.

.... b. were an important location on the trading route.

.... c. came around 1,000 BC or earlier.

.... d. were found in Gran Canaria and Tenerife.

.... e. conquered the islands.

4 Who was it? Tick (✓) the correct column.

	The Spanish	The Guanches
1 They were the first people to live on the Canary Islands.		
2 They were originally from the north of Africa.		
3 They invented the *pintadera*.		
4 They arrived on Tenerife in the 15th century.		
5 They own the Canary Islands today.		

MINI TASK

Choose one of the Canary Islands. Search the Internet for information about the location, population, climate, nature and industry on the island. Write a paragraph about the island and read it to the class.